Star Struck

Street Dance

by Cathy West

StarStruck

Street Dance

by Cathy West

Illustrated by Megan Davidson at Candyreef

Published by Ransom Publishing Ltd.
Radley House, 8 St. Cross Road, Winchester, Hants. SO23 9HX
www.ransom.co.uk

ISBN   978 184167 481 0

First published in 2011

Photographic images copyright ©: cover – Vadym Volodin; pages 4,5 – Izabela Habur; pages 6, 7 – Shad Bolling, NexusMoves, Jeff Medaugh, Paul Kolnik, Konstantin Kamenetskiy; pages 8, 9 – JJRD, Joe Mabel, Cam Vilay, Pixel Addict; pages 10, 11 – Alexander Yakovlev, NexusMoves; pages 12, 13 – Jonas Van Remoortere, Ventobb, Sry85, Manfred Werner – Tsui, Philip Litevsky; pages 14, 15 – boltron, Chris Kirkman, Stealcityrecords, Daniel Lobo, Ray Roper, AngMoKio, leigh awesome, Andrew Braithwaite, Shinjiro; pages 16, 17 – Barbara Henry, che, AngMoKio, Ville Miettinen; black satin, passim – Jon Helgason.

Street Dance

Contents

All About Street Dance

What is street dance?

'Street dance' is all the kinds of dance that happens on the streets, or in parks, school playgrounds or nightclubs.

 You won't see street dance in concert halls or theatres. That's where you go to see ballet, or modern dance.

B-boy Pumba dancing in The Bronx, New York.

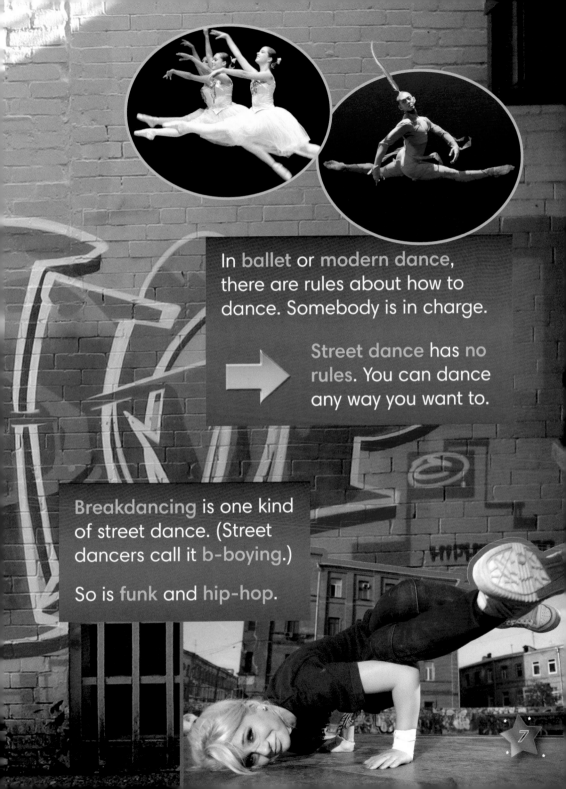

In **ballet** or **modern dance**, there are rules about how to dance. Somebody is in charge.

Street dance has no rules. You can dance any way you want to.

Breakdancing is one kind of street dance. (Street dancers call it b-boying.)

So is funk and hip-hop.

Dance styles

B-boying

Tip: Don't call it breakdancing. Real street dancers never use that name.

Also called breaking. Started in New York City, in the USA, in the 1970s. It is sometimes called hip-hop dance.

The dancers are called b-boys, b-girls, or breakers.

Tecktonik

Also called electro dance. Started in Paris, France. Similar to jumpstyle.

Melbourne shuffle

(or just 'The shuffle'.) Started in Melbourne, Australia. Rapid movement of the toes and heels.

House dance

Started in nightclubs in the USA. Dancers dance to house, disco or techno music.

Jumpstyle

Started at raves and dance clubs in Belgium. It's now popular all over Europe.

Jumpstyle. Really!

9

Dance moves

Popping

When a dancer pops, they jerk their body quickly.

The movements they make are called pops, or hits.

Locking

When a dancer freezes in one position, it's called a lock.

Waving

When a dancer's body ripples, like a wave.

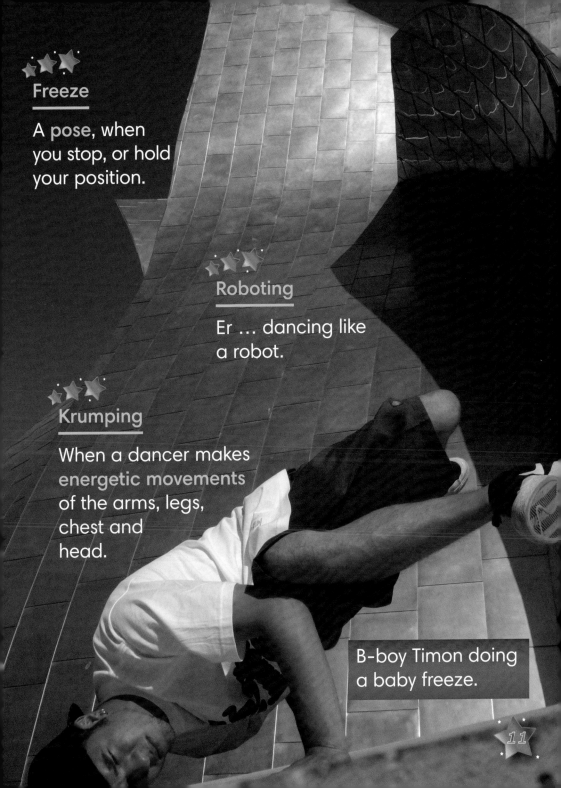

Freeze

A pose, when you stop, or hold your position.

Roboting

Er ... dancing like a robot.

Krumping

When a dancer makes energetic movements of the arms, legs, chest and head.

B-boy Timon doing a baby freeze.

Dance battles

Dance competitions, or dance battles, are an important part of street dance.

Two dancers, or two groups of dancers, try to out-dance each other.

Judges decide who is the winner.

Three members of the hip-hop crew **Multitaskingsistas.**

Crews

Groups of dancers are often called crews.

Famous crews include the Rock Steady Crew, Super Crew and Shebang!

The all-girl crew Shebang!

13

Street dance is everywhere

Street dance is very popular.

- You can see it in **music videos** on MTV.

- You can see it in **TV adverts**.

- You can see it in the **movies**.

- You can see it on **YouTube**.

- You can see it in **nightclubs** and at **raves**.

You can even see it on **postage stamps**.

33
USA

Hip-hop

14

You can see it at dance studios.

Of course, you can see it on the streets, too.

In Japan you can see street dance every Sunday in Yoyogi Park in Tokyo.

15

Street dance has **no rules**. There is no right way to do it. There is no wrong way to do it.

So whatever you do – it's OK!

 But you can learn from others, too.

There are lots of moves that you can use in your dancing:

- Headspins
- Pops
- Locks
- Ripples

Hahny does a headspin.

YouTube is a good place to learn street dance moves.

Many street dancers upload videos of themselves to YouTube.

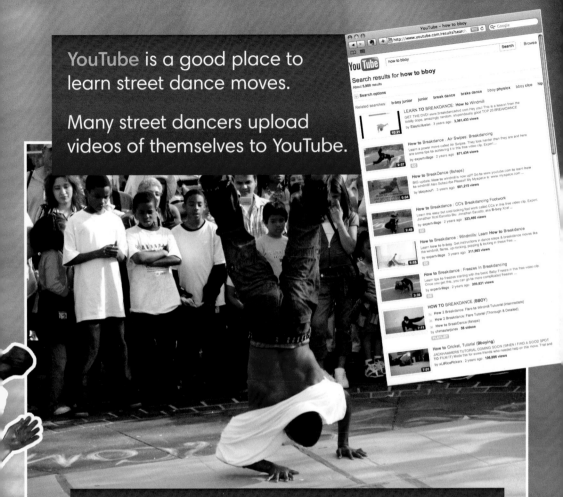

What's the easiest way to be a better dancer?

Practise. Then practise some more.

Why not form a crew with your mates?

Street dance is good exercise too! It keeps your body strong.

Chapter One

The challenge

Kelly met her friend Liz at the park. Kelly had some great new tunes on her iPod. She couldn't wait to play them to Liz.

'You've got to listen to this,' she told Liz. She turned up the volume on her iPod.

'Wow! That's great.' Liz body-popped in time to the music. Kelly joined in. They practised their best hip-hop moves. Kelly was a great dancer.

Then Bob arrived.

Kelly stopped. 'Oh, no! Not Bob,' she moaned. Bob thought he was a great hip-hop dancer.

'I thought I'd find you here,' Bob said. 'I saw your Mum waiting for you outside school.'

'Are you sure?' asked Kelly.

'Ignore him,' Liz said. 'He's probably making it up because he's not as good a dancer as you.'

Bob laughed. 'Oh, yes I am! And I'll prove it. I challenge you to a street dance battle.'

Chapter Two

Caught out

'I accept your challenge,' Kelly said.

But then it started to rain.

'Look, it's raining too hard now. You'll have to have your battle tomorrow,' said Liz.

'OK. First thing tomorrow morning. It's on!' Bob said.

They bumped fists on the deal. Then Kelly rushed home in the rain.

When Kelly got in, her mum was waiting.

'Where have you been?' her mum demanded.

'Maths club,' Kelly said.

'Don't lie to me, Kelly. I went to the school to pick you up and you weren't there. I spoke to your teacher. He told me you haven't been to maths club all term.'

Kelly looked at the floor. She scuffed her feet on the carpet.

Chapter Three

Sneaking about

'Where were you?' Mum asked again.

'I've been dancing in the park with Liz.'

'You what? You're wasting your time dancing. What about your studies?'

'I knew you'd say that. That's why I never told you.'

Kelly stomped up the stairs and slammed her bedroom door.

The next morning, mum knocked on Kelly's bedroom door.

'Are you awake, Kelly?'

There was no answer.

Kelly's mum opened the door. Kelly wasn't there.

'I bet she's gone to the park to dance, even though I told her not to.'

She rushed to her car and sped to the park.

Chapter Four

Battle it out

At the park, Kelly was in the middle of the dance battle against Bob. A big crowd was watching and cheering them on.

Kelly flipped, dropped, spun and glided to her feet.

Next it was Bob's turn. He flipped, spun around on his shoulders and leapt back up in one smooth movement. He added a back flip. The music thumped and his body stayed in perfect time.

Kelly was about to take her turn again. Then she spotted her mum in the crowd.

'Mum! What are you doing here?' Kelly said.

Some of the crowd began to join in with the street dancing.

Kelly's mum started to do the robot. 'This is fun,' she said.

Kelly blushed. 'Mum! Stop!'

'Hey you're good!' Bob said to Kelly's Mum. He started to do the robot too.

'I think you should win the battle,' he said.

Curtain Call

b-boying

b-boys

b-girls

ballet

breakdancing

breakers

breaking

crew

electro dance

funk

headspin

hip-hop

house dance

jumpstyle

krumping

liquid

lock, locking

Melbourne shuffle

modern dance

nightclub

pop, popping

roboting

Rock Steady Crew

Shebang!

tecktonik

theatre

The Bronx

waving

YouTube

Yoyogi Park, Tokyo